Embrace Of Sweet Tomorrows

Sagor sarker

Published by Sagor Sarker, 2024.

EMBRACE OF SWEET TOMORROWS

First edition. November 17, 2024.

ISBN: 979-8230481195

Written by Sagor sarker.

Also by Sagor sarker

The Poetry of Lover's Heart
The Rise of Darkness
Love in Quiet Tremors
The Last Breath of a Love
Embrace Of Sweet Tomorrows
A Smile of Betrayal- A Novel

Watch for more at https://www.facebook.com/sagor.sarker.334/.

Embrace Of Sweet Tomorrows

Love is a journey that takes us on a path filled with twists and turns, highs and lows. It's a feeling that consumes us, fills our hearts, and makes us whole. It's a bond that grows stronger with each passing day, and a flame that burns brighter with every moment we spend together.

In the presence of love, time stands still, and the world fades away. It's a force that can conquer all, even the most insurmountable of obstacles. It's a feeling that can transform us, inspire us, and make us believe in the impossible.

This poem is a celebration of love, a tribute to the power it holds over us, and a testament to the strength it gives us to overcome even the most difficult of challenges. It's a journey through the highs and lows of love, the ups and downs of passion, and the beauty of intimacy.

By- Sagor Sarker

Journey of Love

In your eyes, the constellations burn,
a map of the infinite,
their light spilling secrets into my veins.
Your touch is the sun,
not the meek dawn,
but the fierce, unyielding blaze of noon.

Your love moves through me
like the tide, relentless and ancient,
a song older than the mountains,
its rhythm carving rivers into stone,
etching eternity in the fragile chambers of my heart.
You are the root of my being,
the other wing of this flight,
the shadow that follows even in darkness.
Together, we are a tree growing through the cracks of the world,
its branches breaking open the heavens.

EMBRACE OF SWEET TOMORROWS

Take my hand—no,
take my very breath, my pulse, my name.
Let us walk this earth,
not as mortals,
but as something greater:
an echo of the sea,
a flame defying the wind.

Forever Unfolding Love

My beloved, the rhythm of my life,
each breath I draw is a song of you,
each moment unfurls like the petals of a rose
opening to the sun's quiet insistence.

You are the golden thread of the day,
the scattered stars that whisper my path in the dark.
Your laughter is a river,
carving joy into the cliffs of my solitude,
your smile, a bloom that conquers winter.
In your arms, I am a still see—
no storm, no tide can shake me.
In your gaze, I see the fragile geometry of tomorrow,
a life mapped in the lines of your hands.

EMBRACE OF SWEET TOMORROWS

You are the woman I will grow old beside,
the orchard of my years,
where time ripens into sweetness.
My love for you will never wane—
it is the steadfast moon in a restless sky,
the eternal fire the stars dared us to touch.
You are my heartbeat, my endless song,
and my soul is yours, forever unfolding.

Where the Evening Breaks

The sun dissolves into a trembling sea,
Its golden throat slit by the horizon's edge.
I trace your shadow—fragile, fleeting,
Against the drape of dusk, your shape undone.

You were the blush in the rose of my ribcage,
Each petal aching, unfurling for you.
Now, I gather them in trembling hands,
A bouquet of loss pressed to my chest.
Your voice still lingers like smoke in an empty room,

EMBRACE OF SWEET TOMORROWS

Curling softly, whispering my name.
But silence, a cold lover, claims me now—
Its hands colder than yours ever were.
Oh, how cruel the night,
To stretch its velvet cloak between us.
I ache to stitch its stars together—
A thread of hope, fragile, breaking in my hands.
If I could, I'd carve a door in the moonlight
To find you where time falters,
Where the rivers reverse their flow
And sorrow is just a dream we wake from.
But here, love bleeds out softly,
Pooling in the folds of my dress.
I loved you—
And in the hollow of that love, I still do.

The Fragile Hour

The clock sighs softly, its hands trembling,
Marking moments I can no longer hold.
You were the light that spilled through my windows,
Now shadows stretch where you once stood.

I press my cheek to the ghost of your voice,
A melody faint, unraveling in the air.
It was love, wasn't it?
A fragile thing, cupped between our palms,
Crushed too soon by the weight of our wanting.

EMBRACE OF SWEET TOMORROWS

I still feel you in the cracks of the floorboards,
The spaces where words used to linger.
Your name, a quiet storm behind my lips,
Breaks me like glass every time I speak it.
I would give this breath, this blood,
To find you in the places I can't reach.
But love has no map, no compass to guide—
Only a trail of tears where memories hide.
Tonight, I'll wear this ache like a shroud,
Fold myself into the hollows you left behind.
Perhaps in dreams, I'll find you again—
Whole and laughing, untouched by time.

A Room Without You

This room has grown too large in your absence,
Each wall an echo, a witness to despair.
I run my fingers along the dusted edges,
Searching for the shape of your hands,
The warmth that once lived here.

Do you remember the rain?
How it kissed the windows as we kissed each other,
Our love a storm we couldn't calm.
Now, the rain is quieter,

And I am left listening to its lonely hymn.
I cannot unloved you—
You are the marrow of my thoughts,
The pulse that beats in my silences.
Even in your absence, you are too much here.
I breathe, but the air cuts like glass.
I speak, but the words dissolve into grief.
I sleep, but only to dream of your face,
Only to wake and find it gone.
If love is a wound, let it not heal,
For even pain carries your name.
I would rather ache forever than forget
The way your eyes held the universe still.

Your Breath, My Grave

Your breath once filled this house,
A soft whisper across the lonely wood.
Now the walls lean closer,
Cracked with longing,
Their silence louder than the storms you calmed.

I wear your absence like a winter coat,
Heavy on my shoulders, fraying at the seams.
The wind presses its cold mouth to mine,
But it is not you.

You, who knew how to kiss me alive,.
I plant flowers in the garden of your memory,
But they bloom too brightly,
Mocking the gray of my grief.
Why does beauty linger when love does not?
Why does my heart keep beating
When you are its every reason?

A Love That Forgot Its Name

We once spoke a language no one could understand,
Our voices weaving a tapestry of us.
But now, the threads unravel,
The words dissolve like smoke.

I try to remember the shape of your name
As it fell from my lips,
Soft, tender, trembling with devotion.
Now it tastes foreign,
As if the years have stolen even this.
Love is not cruel, they say—
But they never told me it forgets.
How it slips through the cracks of time,
Falling apart like a brittle photograph
Left too long in the sun.
Still, I hold the pieces close,

EMBRACE OF SWEET TOMORROWS

Press them to my chest,
Hoping their jagged edges might
Reshape into you.

The Place We Left Ourselves

There's a place where we left ourselves,
Half-formed, unfinished,
Like a song caught between verses.
It waits in the corner of a forgotten street,
Its cobblestones worn by time and tears.

I return there sometimes in dreams,
Where the air is thick with you,
And your hand feels warm in mine.
But dawn comes too soon,
And the dream shatters like fragile glass.

EMBRACE OF SWEET TOMORROWS

Was it love, or was it longing,
That tied us so tightly together?
Now, the knot lies undone,
A string without a purpose,
A path without an end.
I cannot rebuild the house we burned,
But I still stand in its ashes,
Waiting for you to return
To the ruin we called home.

A Letter Never Sent

I wrote you a letter last night,
The ink trembling on the page.
Each word a ghost,
Each sentence a wish I cannot speak aloud.

I told you how the nights still ache for you,
How the stars feel like strangers
Without your eyes to reflect them.
I told you how the world turns
But leaves me behind,
Caught in the orbit of your memory.

EMBRACE OF SWEET TOMORROWS

The letter lies folded,
Its edges soft from my touch.
I will not send it,
For where you are,
No words can reach.
Still, I press it to my lips,
A prayer to the universe—
That somewhere, in the spaces between,
You can feel its weight,
And know I loved you enough to never let go.

The Sound of Your Leaving

I heard you leave long before you spoke it,
The quiet unraveling in your voice,
The pause where love used to linger.

Your steps echoed like a drumbeat of endings,
Each one pulling you farther,
Each one pulling me apart.
I stood still, my heart a slow decay,
Watching the door swallow your shadow.
Now, every sound reminds me of you—

EMBRACE OF SWEET TOMORROWS

The rain against the window,
The hum of the kettle,
Even my own breath feels borrowed.
And yet, in this symphony of loss,
I still hear your laughter, faint and far.
A cruel melody, playing on repeat.
I cover my ears, but it follows me,
A song I cannot forget.

The Uncharted Journey

My beautiful wife, my heart is your shore,
where tides rise and fall only in the rhythm of your name.
Each day, my love renews itself,
like a river carving its path through stone,
relentless, eternal.

You are the light that threads through my shadows,

the sudden burst of dawn that blinds the night.
Your smile breaks the sky open—
a quiet fire, a song of warmth,
while your touch whispers across my skin,
a breeze that carries the scent of spring.
To stand beside you is to live within a dream,
a garden suspended in the clouds,
where every leaf holds the secret of our joy.
In your eyes, I find the language of love:
a fierce, unshaken truth that roots itself in the earth.
You are the arc of my existence,
my soul's quiet refrain,
the thread that binds the scattered stars of my being.
My beautiful wife, I will carry you in the marrow of my bones,
in the pulse of my blood,
in the soft hymn of my breath.
You are my beginning and my end,
my forever, my bliss.

The Echoes of Our Memories

Tears fall, each one a shard of the sky breaking,
as your absence pours through me like rain,
drenching the silence with its weight.
I think of you, and the sigh escapes me,
a whisper torn from the roots of my soul.

My heart aches with the delicate fragments of us,
a love fragile yet unyielding,

rare as the bloom of a desert flower.
The nights stretch endlessly, heavy with shadows,
and I call your name into the hollow dark—
it vanishes, unanswered, into the void.
Without you, life is a storm unbound,
rushing forward, untethered, chaotic.
My soul is a ruin, my spirit ash—
the echo of your laughter lingers,
a ghost among the ruins.
I yearn to hold you again,
to trace the map of your touch across my skin,
to anchor myself in the warmth of your arms
and forget this unbearable cold.
But you are gone, and I wander,
adrift in a world made strange,
its edges sharp with loneliness.
So I cling to the echoes of us,
each memory a fragile thread
woven into the fabric of my longing.
I will carry them, cradle them,
until the day we meet again—
and your love, once lost, makes me whole.

Whispers in the Wind

Fifteen years have passed like waves returning to the sea,
yet our love endures,
an ancient tree rooted in the soil of our souls.
From the moment you appeared,
you were the music I had been searching for,
the song that hums in the marrow of my being.

We have stood against storms,
drenched in the rain's wild embrace,
and still, our love blazed like a fire
refusing to surrender to the wind.
Your smile, even now,
scatters the shadows from my days,
and your love ignites my heart—

a flame the years cannot extinguish.
Through every summit and valley,
we have walked side by side,
our hands clasped in quiet prayer,
our hearts a compass guiding us through the unknown.
This love of ours—untamed, unbroken—
is a poem we write with every glance,
a story written not in ink,
but in the breath between us.
Fifteen years of laughter and longing,
and yet the horizon calls, endless and full.
I am unafraid,
for as long as I breathe, I will love you more.
My sweet Tina,
you are my light, my forever.

The Light Within

The widow moves through her days
as though wading through shadows,
a life once bursting with light
now hollowed by the weight of absence.
Her heart, a vessel heavy with grief,
echoes with the name of the love
she can no longer call aloud.

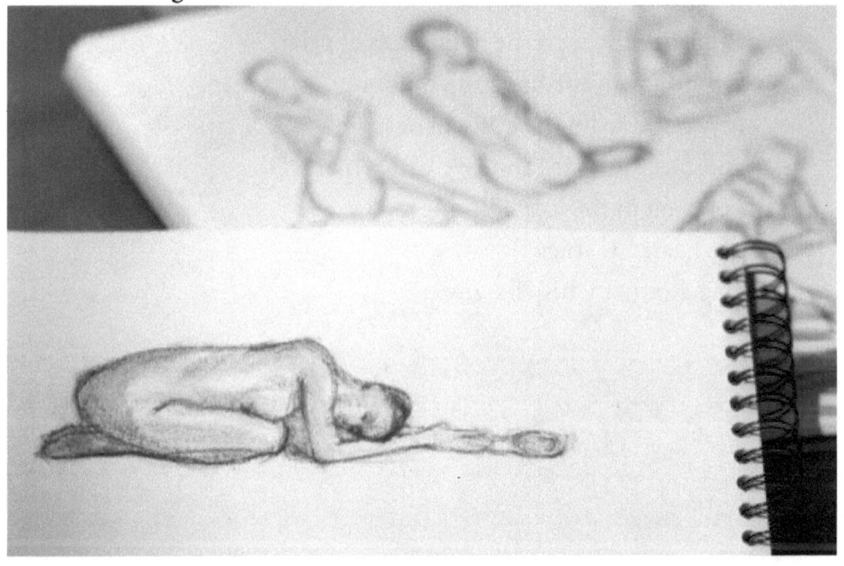

The nights descend, vast and unyielding,
filled only with the murmurs of what was—
the laughter that once adorned the silence,
the warmth of arms
that made even the coldest night bearable.
Yet within her chest,
a fragile ember stirs, refusing to fade,
a stubborn flame fed by memory.
She knows he walks with her still,

his presence a quiet wind
that bends the leaves,
a star that watches from the heavens.
She gathers solace in the fragments,
the gentle weight of their years together—
love woven through the fabric of time,
a love that death could not unravel.
The widow's life is not merely a story
of loss, nor a hymn to her sorrow.
It is a tapestry of resilience,
a journey through the wilderness of grief,
to find joy in the lingering sunlight,
to rebuild from the ashes of despair
and carry forward the love that remains.
For even in the vast emptiness,
she hears his voice,
an echo that whispers: *live.*

Love Knows No Distance

This love of ours defies the map—
it stretches beyond borders,
a flame leaping across the vast expanse of miles.
Distance, that cruel mirage,
cannot sever the threads that bind us,
for love is the rhythm that pulses
in the chambers of our hearts.

Our love is a wildfire,
its embers fierce against the night.
Even when shadows fall between us,
it burns, undimmed, unyielding,
a light that cannot be extinguished.
Every call, every word spoken

across the void,
becomes a lifeline,
a bridge to carry my heart to yours.
With each moment of connection,
my soul rises,
as though the distance itself were vanquished.
No horizon can silence this love,
no ocean can swallow its song.
It is unbreakable,
woven from the stars
and the breath of the earth,
stronger than time or space.
So let us keep this fire alive,
tend it with every memory, every hope.
One day, the distance will collapse into nothing,
and we will stand together,
a constellation whole once more.
Until that day, my love,
I carry you within me—
a light unwavering,
a warmth that endures every shadow.
For wherever we are,
our hearts remain as one.

Love Eternal

Age is a shadow, fleeting and pale,
a whisper against the roar of our love.
The heart knows no years,
its rhythm eternal,
beating only for you, my infinite song.

With each year that passes,
my love for you deepens,
like roots entwining beneath the earth—
a bond unshaken by the winds of time.
You are my completion,

the melody that threads through my silence,
the star that rises in my darkest skies.
The lines that trace my face,
the silver woven in my hair,
are not marks of loss but of living—
a life shaped by your love's radiant presence.
These wrinkles are the rivers
carved by laughter and longing,
proof that our love has weathered
all the storms of this world.
Your touch still awakens the earth within me,
your smile, a sun that melts my doubts.
Even now, my heart trembles as it did
the first time I knew your name,
the first time I dared to hope
you might be mine.
So take my hand,
and let us walk this road together,
each step a testament to the love we've built.
With you beside me,
the weight of the years is nothing but a feather,
and the journey ahead
is boundless, infinite, ours.

Young Love's Magic

The butterflies inside me stir—
a soft, trembling storm
with each heartbeat that whispers your name.
This love is a fire,
pure and unbound,
lifting my soul into realms
I had only dreamed of.

Your smile is the sun's first light,
breaking open the day.
When your gaze meets mine,
the world dissolves,
and I melt into the warmth
only your presence can bring.
You are the laughter that ripples
through the still waters of my days,
the quiet understanding that wraps itself

around the chaos of my thoughts.
You hold my burdens
as though they were feathers.
Being with you is alchemy,
a transformation—
the ordinary turned to gold.
You are not a dream,
but a reality so radiant,
it feels like magic stitched into my life.
Let us hold this love as the treasure it is,
a spark to illuminate every shadow.
With you,
every step becomes lighter,
every horizon within reach.
Together, we will write our days into eternity,
one moment at a time.

The First Time

The first time I saw you,
my heart shattered and soared,
as if the universe itself paused—
holding its breath
so it could witness the miracle of you.
In that single instant,
I knew my life had been incomplete
until the moment you stepped into it,
and you filled every empty corner with light.

Your beauty was not the fleeting kind,
but something eternal—
a light that pierced through all the darkness,
a warmth that ignited the deepest parts of me
I never knew could burn.
And the kindness in your eyes—
it was a soft revolution,
changing everything,
turning me into someone new.
You stood by me when the world became too heavy,
lifting me with a touch,
a word,
a quiet strength that poured into me
when I thought I could no longer stand.
And every time I stumbled,
you became my reason to rise,
the voice that told me
there was more to live for.
You were the first to show me what love could be,
its depth, its weight,
its quiet power that filled the spaces between us
and wrapped itself around my soul.
You were the first to hold my hand,
the first to kiss me,
and in that kiss,
I tasted forever.
Together, we've built something so much greater
than love itself—
a life that echoes with laughter and tears,
a world woven from the threads of our hearts.
With every day we share,
I fall deeper into you,

into the rhythm of your breath,
into the space where only we exist,
and my heart beats faster,
quicker,
as if it's been waiting for this forever.
So let us raise a glass to that first moment,
the one where everything changed.
For you are not just my love—
you are my beginning,
my endless,
my forever.

Teenage Lovebirds

In the corridors of youth,
where books lay heavy with dreams
and rules whispered like distant storms,
our love began—
wild and untamed,
a bloom in the garden of reckless hearts.

Your smile was the sunrise
that broke through the mundane,
and your laugh—
oh, how it sang like the wind through open windows,
stirring the air and the soul.
Every glance, every brush of your hand,
sent my heart into a trembling dance,
as if it had never known such joy.
We found secret corners
where the world couldn't follow,
where our kisses—new and trembling—
were the promises of eternity,

and in the cradle of each other's arms,
we discovered a love too pure
to be caught by the passing hours.
Through proms and football games,
the bright chaos of teenage dreams,
our love grew like the roots of an old tree,
unseen but steady,
a force that shaped us
with every season.
Now those days are ghosts,
their echoes fading beneath the weight of time,
but our love—
it has only deepened,
a river flowing stronger with every year,
its current unstoppable,
its waters boundless.
So let us drink to the days of youth,
to the first bloom of our hearts.
For though the halls of school have crumbled,
our love will never fade—
it will burn,
and burn,
and burn,
until we are nothing but light.

College Sweethearts

In the halls of youth, we met—
    two souls, bright and unafraid,
    entwined in the tapestry of destiny.
    We shared our wildest dreams,
    our fears whispered in the quiet moments,
    and in the laughter that spilled like rain,
    we learned the language of love.

Together, we walked beneath the endless sky,
hand in hand, across the green campus,

through rooms filled with knowledge and questions,
but our hearts, untamed,
were already writing their own story.
In the stillness of side-by-side study,
our love grew like a vine,
climbing with every glance,
reaching farther than the walls of classrooms.
We sought secret corners,
places where the world could not intrude,
where our deepest thoughts were shared
with the tenderness of first words.
And in those stolen moments,
we found the purity of a love
so soft, yet so fierce,
that even time could not hold it still.
Those college days—
they fled like birds from a cage,
but our love,
it lingered,
rooted in the soil of time,
its strength becoming the foundation of all we are.
So let us raise a glass to the days of youth,
to the fire that first sparked between us,
for though the seasons of college have passed,
our love, like the stars above,
will forever burn—
a flame that knows no end.

Next Door Love

In quiet moments, day by day,
I never thought that love would stray
into the path where I reside—
but fate, in its own way, did guide.
Each morning in the yard we met,
a wave, a glance, so brief, so set,
yet slowly, as the days passed by,
a deeper spark began to fly.

We sat upon the porch at night,
beneath the stars' soft, trembling light,
and spoke of dreams that lingered still,
of hopes we held, our hearts to fill.
And with each word, our bond did grow,
a love as deep as rivers flow,

until we walked the block, hand clasped,
in laughter that time could not outlast.
Now side by side, where once we stood,
our love, unspoken, understood—
for more than neighbors we remain,
soulmates bound by love's sweet chain.

Unexpected Love's Journey

Love, like a shadow in the night,
Comes softly, without hint or light,
And changes all in ways unknown,
Turning the heart to make it its own.

I sought not love, nor did I wait,
But when you entered, it was fate.
Your smile, a beacon in the gloom,
Your laugh, a song that filled the room.
Each moment spent with you did fly,
And every glance made spirits rise.
We spoke of things both deep and bright,
And in your voice, my heart took flight.
We shared our dreams, our hopes, our fears,
And built a bond that through the years
Would grow, like vines in summer's sun,
And carry us till life's race is run.

Through trials faced, we did not break,
For love, unexpected, we did take
And made it bloom, both wild and true,
A journey made for me and you.
Now, hand in hand, through paths unknown,
We walk, together—never alone.
Though love arrived as unbidden grace,
It is the finest gift life could embrace.

Second Chance at Love

In the bloom of life, when years have passed,
We found a love, both slow and vast—
A mid-age romance, tender and true,
A heart's revival, old yet new.

We had lived and learned, seen joys and strife,
But still, the hunger for love was rife.
By chance we met, and in that instant,
Our hearts took flight, so pure, persistent.
We spoke for hours, beneath the moon's pale light,
Of days gone by and dreams in sight.

In the weave of laughter, joy, and tears,
We found a bond that calmed our fears.
Each dawn brought love that grew, and thrived,
In every glance, our spirits dived
Into a future, rich and bright,
Where together we would take flight.
A second chance, this love so sweet,
A journey where our hearts could meet.
We cherish each moment, each stolen glance,
A dance of love, a second chance.
So here's to love, both deep and wise,
To the joy that fills our weary eyes.
Hand in hand, we walk the road—
And in our hearts, true love we've sowed.

A Love Born of Friendship

In friendship's depths, where hearts are bound,
A love emerges, pure, profound.
Beyond the reach of words and time,
A sacred bond, a love sublime.

In moments shared, both light and dark,

Through every hope and whispered spark,
Our hearts beat in a quiet song,
A love that grows, so deep, so strong.
Our friendship—an unwavering base,
Built on trust, with gentle grace.
But with each passing dawn's soft hue,
A love, more tender, slowly grew.
The warmth of you, your tender touch,
Fills my soul with joy, so much.
In the gaze of your knowing eyes,
Lies love, no mask, no sweet disguise.
So let us hold this love so dear,
That bloomed from friendship, crystal-clear.
A love that's deep, a love that's true,
Found not in chance, but me and you.

Forever My Cherished Wife

My love, my life, my cherished bride,
In thee, my heart does swell with pride.
For every moment, tender, true,
Is made complete by one like you.

You are the light that guides my way,
In darkest hours, you lead the day.
Your gentle touch, your soul's embrace,
Fill me with joy, a boundless grace.
Your beauty, not in form alone,
But in the love your spirit's shown.

Your smile, like dawn's first golden hue,
Makes every day more bright, anew.
Grateful am I, for every breath,
For in your love, I've found no death.
With you, beside me, I behold
A world of blessings, rich and bold.
My soulmate, partner, dearest friend,
My love for you shall never end.
So let these whispered words declare,
My love for you, forever fair.
Through thick and thin, I'll hold your hand,
Together, love will ever stand.
My love, my life, my cherished wife,
You are my world, my soul, my life.

The Echoes of Silence

The love we shared, once sweet, now cold,
A tale of passion, silent, bold.
In shadows deep, it fades away,
Leaving me lost, in endless dismay.

I thought our hearts would never part,
But now, it feels as though they start
To tear asunder, rift by rift,
A love once pure, now lost to drift.
I miss the sound of tender laugh,
The whispered joy, the tender craft—
Now silence reigns, a hollow sound,
Where once our love did sweetly drown.
I long to turn the hands of time,
To fix the cracks, the broken rhyme,
But fate, it seems, has closed its door,
And love's embrace is ours no more.

So here I stand, amidst the cold,
With memories, once bright, now old.
Though love has died, a scar remains,
A lingering shadow, endless pains.
I cherish, though, each fleeting glance,
Each moment lost, each broken dance.
For though our love has ceased to be,
It haunts the hollow heart of me.

The Symphony of Silence

My heart, a heavy stone, does weigh,
And numbed, my thoughts begin to stray.
I never thought this fate would come,
A love once bright now turned to none.

The memories surge, both dark and light,
Each one a ghost that haunts the night.

I mourn the laughter, the tender sighs,
Now lost beneath the void of lies.
Though time may soothe this shattered soul,
In this moment, I'm but a hollow toll.
The distance grows, yet still you linger,
A shadow that haunts with trembling finger.
I seek escape, a fresh rebirth,
Yet all I find is empty earth.
For now, my tears shall freely fall,
As silence echoes through this hall.
Farewell to love, now lost in time,
I leave behind this bitter rhyme.
Yet as I turn and fade from view,
A piece of me will always stay with you.

Widowed, Yet Never Alone

Alone in silence, she weeps and weeps,
Her soul adrift in sorrow's deep.
The love she knew, now torn and gone,
Left her to wander, broken, alone.

The years they spent, once sweet and bright,
Now fading dim like dying light.
Her heart, a hollow tomb of ache,
Longs for the touch she cannot take.
The memory of him haunts her still,
A shadow that time cannot kill.
She clings to what they used to share,
A fleeting dream, now trapped in air.
Each day, a wound that never heals,
A lover's death, a wound that steals.
Her heart, a hollow shell of grief,
Wanders in shadows, seeking brief relief.

Yet, in the darkness, she finds her way,
For love, though gone, will never stray.
His spirit whispers soft and low,
And in her soul, his love will grow.
The tears may fall, the ache remain,
But death's cruel grasp cannot restrain.
For though he's gone from earth's embrace,
His love endures, transcends all space.
She'll carry on, her spirit torn,
But in her heart, he'll neer be scorned.
And in the quiet, she'll always find,
Their love, eternal, intertwined.

The Mirror of Us

I look into the mirror,
And it shows me your face instead of mine.
The curve of your smile,
The fire in your eyes—
Once, they lit the rooms of my soul.

But now, the glass is cracked.
Your image splinters into shards,
And I cannot piece you back together.
I try to hold them,

These fragments of us,
But they cut my hands and draw no blood—
Only memories.
If the mirror could speak,
It would ask where you've gone,
And why the silence grows louder with each passing day.
But it is mute, like me,
Left only to reflect
What we've both lost.

Your Shadow Stays

You are not here, but your shadow lingers,
Clinging to the walls like ivy,
Refusing to let go of the spaces you claimed.
I try to sweep it away,
But it curls around my fingers,
A phantom of your touch.

The sunlight is cruel;
It illuminates your absence,
Carving shapes of emptiness where you stood.
Even the moon, soft and forgiving,
Hides its face from me,

Ashamed of its pale imitation of you.
If shadows are echoes of what was,
Then I am haunted,
A house where love once lived,
And grief now resides.

The Edge of Your Name

Your name hangs on the edge of my lips,
Too sharp to speak, too heavy to swallow.
I carry it like a stone in my pocket,
A weight I cannot throw away.

I write it in the frost on the window,
Only to watch it vanish with the morning sun.
I whisper it to the trees,
But the wind carries it somewhere
I cannot follow.

Does your name still taste like mine?
Or has it been washed clean
By the tides of time?
I fear the day it becomes a stranger,
When even its edges no longer cut me.

A Room of Forgotten Things

I found a room today,
Hidden behind a door I hadn't noticed before.
Inside were the pieces of us:
A broken watch, a threadbare scarf,
A photograph with edges curling like autumn leaves.

I touched each thing,
And it touched me back,
Their whispers soft as dying embers.
This is where love goes when it is forgotten,

I thought—
To a room where time stands still,
Where the heart keeps beating
Long after it should.
I left the door ajar,
In case you find it, too.
Perhaps then, we could meet again
Among the fragments of our once.

A Love Without Witness

The world didn't see us,
Didn't mark the nights we lay awake,
Tracing constellations on each other's skin.
It didn't hear the songs we made,
The way our hearts beat in perfect, imperfect rhythm.

But the world saw you leave.
It saw my hands reach for yours,
Grasping at air,
And it called it a tragedy.

I wanted our love to be known,
But not like this—
Not in the silence that followed your footsteps,
Not in the echoes of a door that wouldn't stay closed.
Still, I remember it all.
Our love, quiet but fierce,
A flame no one saw,
But that burned me to ash when it went out.

The Weight of an Empty Chair

Your chair sits by the window,
Its arms stretching toward a sun
It will never feel again.
I drape a blanket across its back,
As if it, too, could grow cold in your absence.

I cannot sit there,
Cannot fill the space where you once were.
The weight of it—light, yet crushing—
Presses against my chest,

A reminder of what remains
And what does not.
The chair does not complain,
But it leans slightly,
As if bending under the burden of waiting.
And I lean with it,
Both of us longing for your return.

END

My name is F. N. M. Komor, but most people know me as *Sagor Sarker*. I'm from Bangladesh, a beautiful country in South Asia. Born on 01November , 1990, I have a background in Management, with both graduate and post-graduate degrees, plus an MBA in Marketing.

Writing has always been my passion, even though it's not my profession. I love reading books and exploring new ideas, and I enjoy sharing my thoughts and stories with others. Through my writing, I aim to connect with readers and bring a bit of my world to theirs.

Author: Sagor Sarker

Email: fnmkomor@gmail.com

Embrace of Sweet Tomorrows

Published by Self-Publishing

Author: Sagor Sarker

Email: fnmkomor@gmail.com

ISBN: 9798230481195

About the Author

My name is F. N. M. Komor, but most people know me as *Sagor Sarker*. I'm from Bangladesh, a beautiful country in South Asia. Born on 01November , 1990, I have a background in Management, with both graduate and post-graduate degrees, plus an MBA in Marketing.

Writing has always been my passion, even though it's not my profession. I love reading books and exploring new ideas, and I enjoy sharing my thoughts and stories with others. Through my writing, I aim to connect with readers and bring a bit of my world to theirs.

Read more at https://www.facebook.com/sagor.sarker.334/.

www.ingramcontent.com/pod-product-compliance
Lightning Source LLC
LaVergne TN
LVHW091223150826
845673LV00003B/991

* 9 7 9 8 2 3 0 4 8 1 1 9 5 *